D1397059

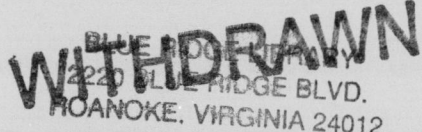

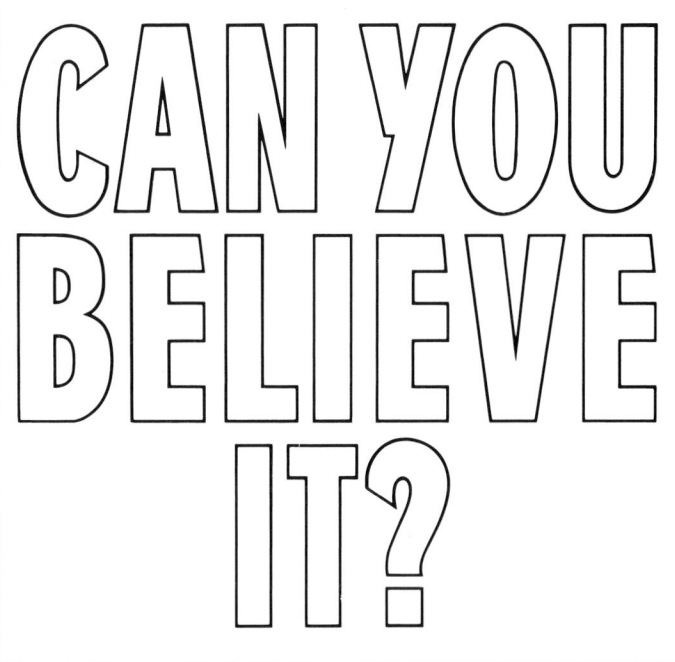

CAN YOU BELIEVE IT?

- THE WORLD OF SCIENCE -

Written by
JENNY VAUGHAN

Illustrated by
SALLIE REASON

Derrydale Books
New York

A TEMPLAR BOOK

This 1990 edition published by Derrydale Books
distributed by Crown Publishers, Inc.,
225 Park Avenue South, New York, New York 10003

Devised and produced by Templar Publishing Company Ltd
Pippbrook Mill, London Road, Dorking, Surrey RH4 1JE,
Great Britain

ISBN 0-517-69907-9
h g f e d c b a

PICTURE CREDITS

Key: Top = t, bottom = b, left = l, right = r

Front cover: l B. Wilson/Sheridan Photo Library; b Dieter and Mary Plage/Bruce Coleman Limited; r NASA/Science Photo Library

Pages 4–5 NASA/Science Photo Library; page 7 Alex Bartel/Science Photo Library; page 8 Heini Schneebeli/Science Photo Library; page 11 Andia National Laboratories/Science Photo Library; page 13 Zefa Picture Library; page 14 Science Photo Library; page 17 Philippe Plailly/Science Photo Library; page 21 David Parker/Science Photo Library; page 22 Alexander Tsiaras/Science Photo Library; page 25 Dieter and Mary Plage/Bruce Coleman Limited; page 26 Northern Ireland Tourist Board; page 29 Earth Satellite Corporation/Science Photo Library; page 30 Nelson Medina/Science Photo Library; page 34 NASA/Science Photo Library.

CONTENTS

1. Is it true that what goes up must come down? 4
2. Is everything made up of tiny atoms? 4
3. Is space full of dust? 4
4. Do metals get tired? 5
5. Can air be heavy? 5
6. What happened to Archimedes in his bath? 6
7. Can light be made to bend? 6
8. How can you make your hair stand on end? 7
9. Can you reflect heat with a mirror? 7
10. Can oil be "cracked?" 8
11. Can you reach the end of a rainbow? 8
12. Is molten iron really poured into pigs? 8
13. Can aircraft fly faster than the speed of sound? 9
14. Can you spin glass? 9
15. Is there life on distant planets? 10
16. Can you drink acid? 10
17. Can you cut metal with a knife? 11
18. Is it possible to split an atom? 11
19. Could you catch a falling star? 12
20. Did the universe start with a huge explosion? 12
21. What are liquid crystals? 13
22. Can you sit on the sea? 13
23. Can a space be completely empty? 13
24. How long does it take the light from distant stars
to reach us? 14
25. Could you take a photo of your insides? 14
26. Do sounds make waves? 15
27. Could a nuclear power station actually melt? 15
28. Is there a metal that is usually a liquid? 16
29. Are there dwarfs in space? 16
30. Can you cut things with light? 16
31. Can you make a three-dimensional picture? 17
32. How can you make a magnet with electricity? 17
33. Could you land an aircraft on an iceberg? 18
34. How much of an iceberg do you actually see? 18
35. Can an aerosol spray make a hole in the
atmosphere? 19
36. Is plastic really made from oil? 19
37. Have we received messages from Mars? 19
38. Will we ever be able to live on the Moon? 20
39. Is the Earth really a huge magnet? 20

40. Can a beam of light play records? 21
41. Can you make gold? 21
42. Does everything fall at the same speed? 21
43. How can clothes be whiter than white? 22
44. Are Egyptian mummies really radioactive? 22
45. Does radiation stay around for ever? 23
46. How can something grow just by getting hot? 23
47. Can you use salt to make ice-cream? 24
48. Can you really make electricity with a lemon? 24
49. Can mountains grow? 25
50. Is it true that lightning never strikes twice in the
same place? 25
51. Is glass really made of sand? 26
52. Who built the Giant's Causeway? 26
53. Can you skate on water? 26
54. How can acid rain from the sky? 27
55. Are charcoal and diamonds really the same
thing? 27
56. How long is a day on the planet Mercury? 28
57. Is the Sun always the same size? 28
58. Can you use radio waves to look at the stars? 29
59. Can you tell if something is warm by looking at
a photograph? 29
60. Can you make yellow from green and red? 30
61. Can a lightning rod really save a building in a
storm? 30
62. How do you change the color of glass? 31
63. How do you use a laser to measure the distance
between the Earth and the Moon? 31
64. Is it possible to destroy something completely? 31
65. Can we wear clothes made of plastic? 32
66. What stops an aircraft from falling out of the sky? 32
67. Will Asia really split in half one day? 33
68. Can you keep water in a glass which is
upside-down? 33
69. What is talcum powder? 34
70. Are all planets made of rock? 34
71. Does the world stay the same temperature? 35
72. Does heat change things for ever? 35
73. Are there really black holes in space? 35
Index 36

1. Is it true that what goes up must come down?

On Earth and on other planets, and even the Moon, a force called **gravity** draws everything down. So anything that goes up will come down again. Without air, everything would fall at the same speed, but here on Earth air makes a difference. Some objects, such as feathers, tend to float in the air, but even they fall down eventually. Only in space, out of the reach of gravity, can something go up and not come down again.

2. Is everything made up of tiny atoms?

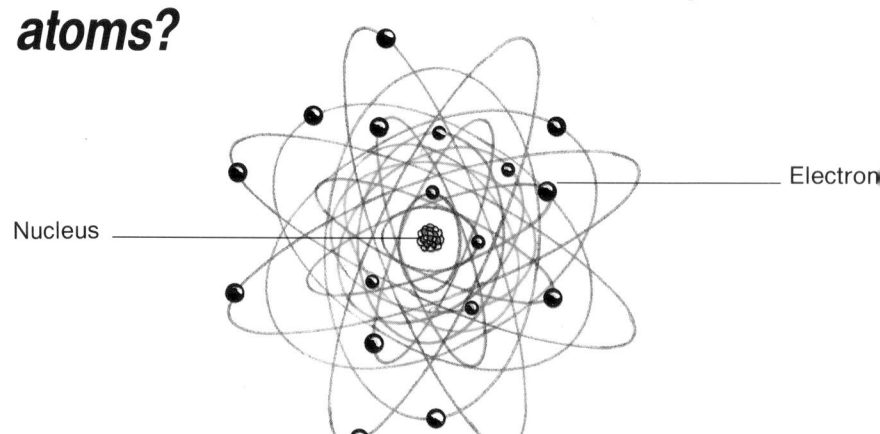

Nucleus

Electron

Everything in the universe is made of tiny particles called **atoms**. They are far too small to see — even the smallest speck of dust contains millions of atoms. Even though atoms are so small, scientists have discovered their structure. Each atom has a central part, called a **nucleus**, which contains particles called **protons**, and usually **neutrons** as well. Tiny particles called **electrons** move around the nucleus.

3. Is space full of dust?

Yes, there are large clouds of dust, mixed with the gas hydrogen, far out in space. They are called **nebulae** (**nebula** is the Latin word for a cloud). Stars are forming inside them. You can see our nearest nebula — the Orion Nebula in the constellation of Orion — through an ordinary telescope. It looks like a dim, misty patch.

4. Do metals get tired?

Yes, metals do get tired. Metals are very strong and can withstand a lot of stress (pulling or bearing weight). However, if they have to bear differing amounts of stress over a long time, they get weaker. If a metal is subjected to vibrations it may crack, especially around any weak spots, such as holes. If a metal becomes so worn that it breaks, we say it has **metal fatigue***. This can be very dangerous. If an aircraft suffers metal fatigue it may break up in mid-air. Aircraft have to be tested carefully and regularly to make sure that any wear is spotted at the earliest possible stage.*

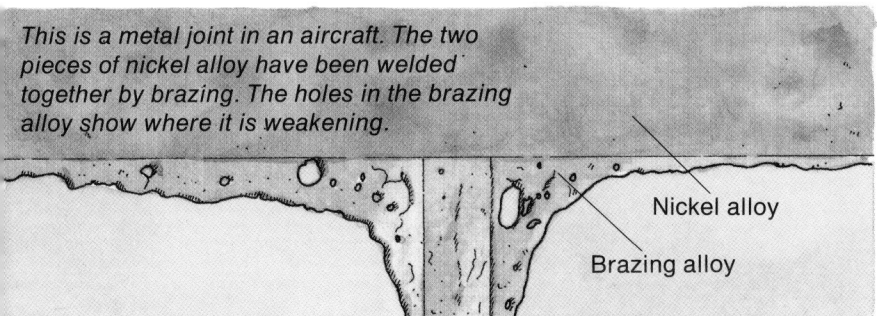

This is a metal joint in an aircraft. The two pieces of nickel alloy have been welded together by brazing. The holes in the brazing alloy show where it is weakening.

Nickel alloy

Brazing alloy

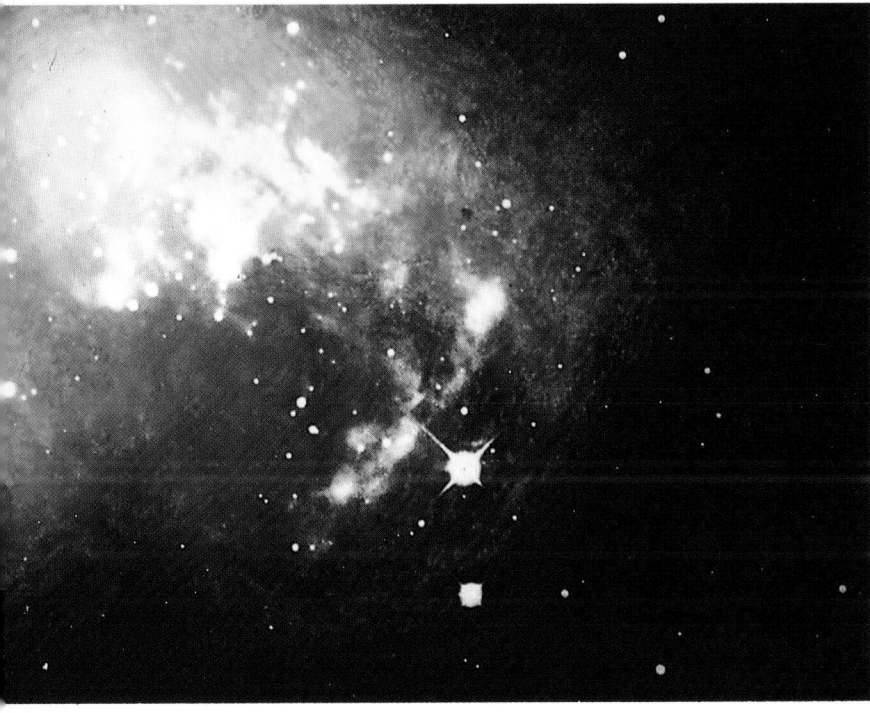

5. Can air be heavy?

We often say that something is as light as air — but air is actually quite heavy. The layer of air around the Earth presses down on the Earth's surface — we say that it is exerting pressure. The column of air pressing down on your head weighs about 1 ton. We cannot feel this air pressure, because the pressure of the air inside our bodies is equal to the pressure of the air outside.

6. What happened to Archimedes in his bath?

Archimedes was a scientist. He lived in Sicily more than 2,000 years ago. He wanted to find out how to measure the volume of an irregularly shaped object. (The volume of something is the space it takes up). He discovered how to do it when he was in his bath. As he jumped in, water spilled over the edge. Archimedes realized that you can figure out an object's volume by seeing how much water it displaces (pushes away). He was so happy when he discovered this that he jumped out of the bath and ran into the street shouting "Eureka!" which means "I've found it!"

EUREKA!

7. Can light be made to bend?

A beam of light will change direction if it passes through a liquid, a lens, or if it meets a mirror. The light does not bend gradually, it suddenly changes the angle at which it is traveling. Light can be made to bend if it travels along very fine tubes of glass, called **fiber optic tubes**. As it travels through the fiber, it is reflected back and forth by the inside surface of the tube. In this way light can be made to bend around corners.

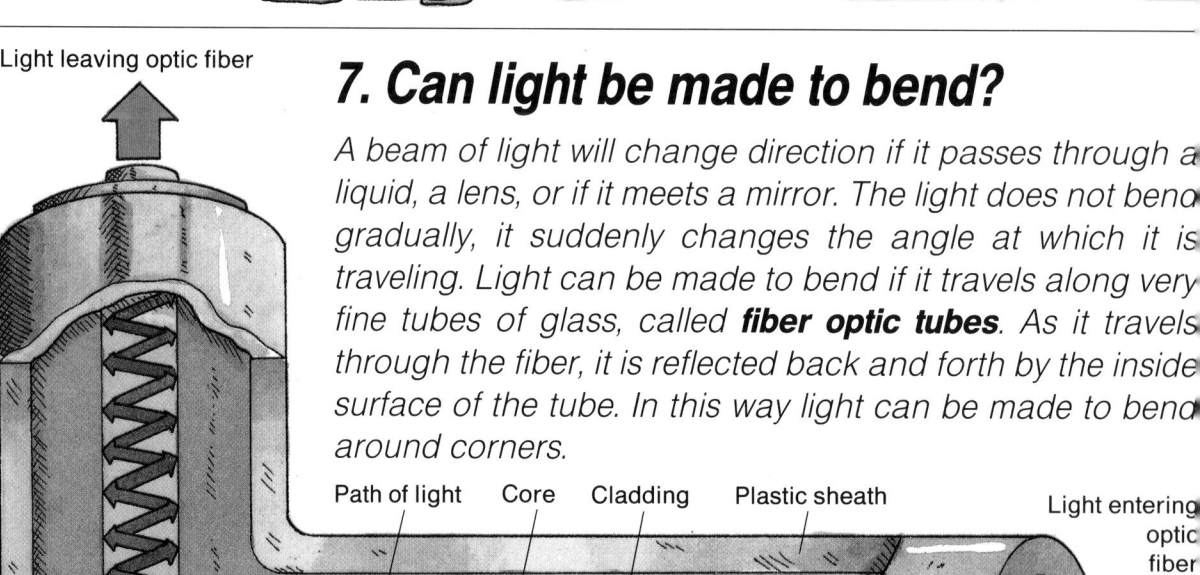

Light leaving optic fiber

Path of light   Core   Cladding   Plastic sheath

Light entering optic fiber

8. How can you make your hair stand on end?

Electricity can make your hair stand on end. If you comb clean hair very hard, the atoms that make up your hair change. Electrons are dislodged from them and cling to the comb, giving it a **negative electrical charge**. Your hair is left with a **positive charge**. Negative charges attract positive charges and so your hair stands up because it is attracted to the comb.

9. Can you reflect heat with a mirror?

Heat and light are both forms of energy — and can be reflected by a mirror. Heat travels in waves called **thermal radiation**. A mirror can be used to redirect these waves. In a solar furnace, huge mirrors are used to reflect heat from the Sun on to a furnace. Some solar furnaces are used to make steam, which drives turbines for generating electricity. This furnace in France can reach a heat of up to 7232°F and melt metals!

10. Can oil be "cracked?"

"Cracking" is a process used to turn heavy, unrefined products into lighter, more useful ones. Thick, heavy crude oil is taken to a refinery, heated and put into a tall tower called a **distillation column**. As it cools down, it separates into different products. Light gas and gasoline are removed from the top of the column, heavy fuel oil and bitumen from the bottom.

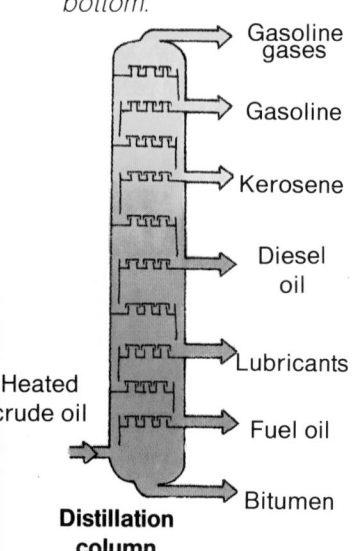

Gasoline gases

Gasoline

Kerosene

Diesel oil

Lubricants

Heated crude oil

Fuel oil

Bitumen

Distillation column

12. Is molten iron really poured into pigs?

Yes, but not the sort of pig that lives in a sty! A "pig" is the name for a mold into which molten iron is drained after it has been melted in a furnace. The name comes from the fact that, in the past, the iron ore was poured into grooves in a bed of sand. These had a main stem with branches coming out of the side. People thought they looked like a sow suckling a row of piglets.

11. Can you reach the end of a rainbow?

A rainbow is formed by sunlight shining through distant raindrops. As we move closer to it, we see the light through different raindrops yet further away. So we can never reach the end of a rainbow!

13. Can aircraft fly faster than the speed of sound?

Sound travels through air at about 745 miles an hour. Concorde, and many other aircraft (mostly military ones) can travel faster than this. We say that they can go at supersonic speeds. When aircraft switch to supersonic power, they create shock waves in the air. These result in a loud, explosive noise called a **sonic boom**.

14. Can you spin glass?

When natural fibers such as wool and cotton are spun, they are twisted together to make long threads out of many short ones. Amazingly, glass can also be spun into thread. First it is melted and then forced through fine holes. These **glass fibers** are then used in telecommunications and to reinforce plastics. They can also be turned into a kind of matting used for insulating attics, as shown here. This prevents heat from escaping through the roof of the house.

Fiberglass insulation

15. Is there life on distant planets?

Scientists are sure that there is no life on the other planets in our solar system. Some are too cold because they are so far from the Sun. Others are too hot. Venus has thick clouds of poisonous sulphuric acid, and space probes show us that there is no life on Mars. But there are other suns in the universe, with other planets around them. They could have life of some kind. Who knows?

16. Can you drink acid?

An acid is a chemical substance that combines with metals to form **salts**. Some acids are very strong and can destroy almost anything. They are dangerous to touch. Other acids are much weaker and a great many can be found in food and drink. We find them in fruit and in anything that tastes sharp, such as vinegar. Many drinks contain citric acid, which is found in lemons, limes, and other citrus fruits.

17. Can you cut metal with a knife?

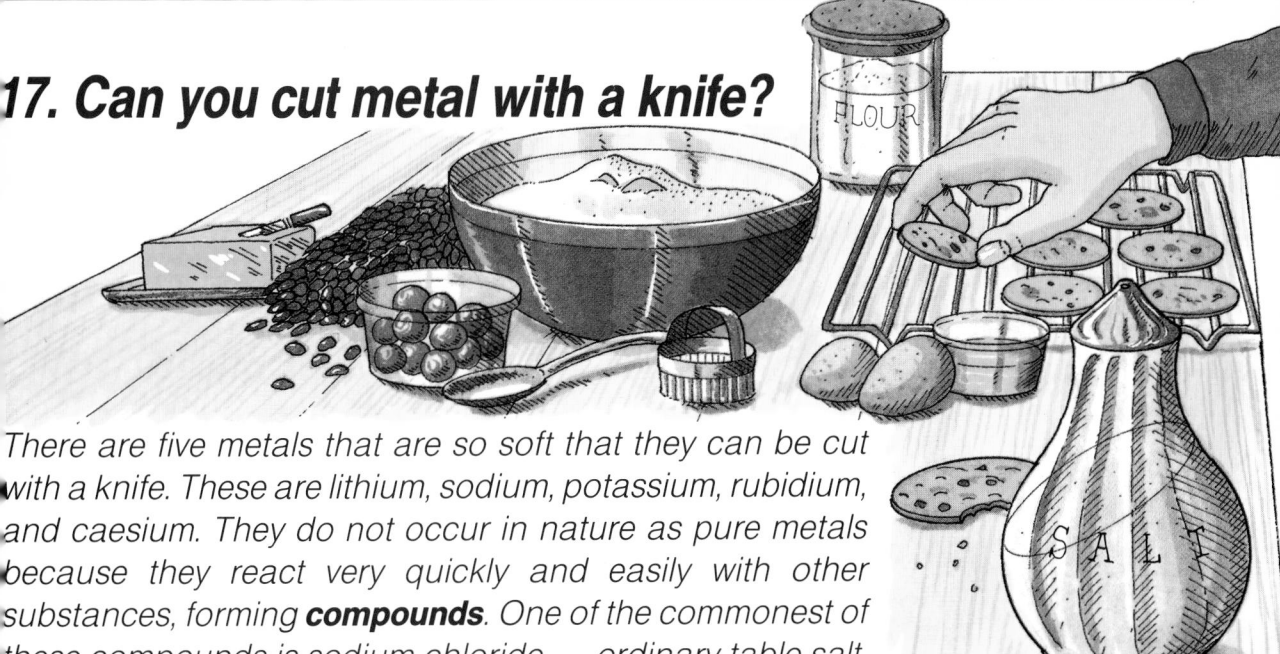

There are five metals that are so soft that they can be cut with a knife. These are lithium, sodium, potassium, rubidium, and caesium. They do not occur in nature as pure metals because they react very quickly and easily with other substances, forming **compounds**. One of the commonest of these compounds is sodium chloride — ordinary table salt.

18. Is it possible to split an atom?

Yes, this process is called **nuclear fission**. It is used in making nuclear power. Uranium atoms are bombarded with neutrons. When a neutron strikes a uranium atom, the nucleus splits in two, releasing yet more neutrons. These neutrons strike more atoms and the process continues in a **chain reaction**. A huge amount of heat energy is released. In a power plant, this heat is used to make steam, which drives turbines. If the reaction gets out of control, there is a huge explosion. This photograph shows the core of a nuclear reactor where nuclear fission takes place.

CAN YOU BELIEVE IT?

19. Could you catch a falling star?

No, because stars do not fall to Earth. Large fragments of rock called **meteorites** sometimes fall to Earth, forming craters. Other tiny fragments of rocks and dust from space, called **meteors**, also fall toward Earth but burn up when they hit the Earth's atmosphere. People often mistakenly call them "shooting stars."

20. Did the universe start with a huge explosion?

No one knows how the universe started. One theory is that i started 15,000 million years ago with a huge explosion — sometimes called the "big bang." The universe grew large and larger, the galaxies forming first, then the stars and planets. Another theory is that there have been a number o "big bangs." The idea is that the universe expands and contracts regularly, with a new big bang about every 80,000 million years. These theories do not tell us very much abou how the universe was formed — or what was there before it We do know that the other galaxies are moving away from us very quickly, so the universe is probably getting bigger But we have no way of knowing what lies beyond it.

21. *What are liquid crystals?*

"Liquid crystals" are molecules (tiny particles) that change shape when an electrical charge passes through them. The crystals lie between two sheets of glass. Normally, light passes through them and so we cannot see them. When an electrical charge is applied, the crystals change shape so that light cannot pass through them. They show up as dark marks. The figures on a watch are formed in this way.

22. *Can you sit on the sea?*

The Dead Sea lies between Israel and Jordan. Although it receives water from seven rivers, it has no outflow. The level of the water is maintained by evaporation. Because of this it is about eight times saltier and therefore much denser, than ordinary sea water. This means that it is better at supporting objects. Our bodies float so well in this very salty water that we can actually float sitting up in it.

23. *Can a space be completely empty?*

*An empty space, without anything in it (even air), is called a **vacuum**. Wherever a vacuum is created, something always rushes to fill it. If you pumped all the air out of a can, the pressure of the air outside would force the walls in and the can would collapse. Glass is stronger. It does not collapse under the pressure. This is why glass is used to create the vacuum in a vacuum bottle. Heat cannot pass through a vacuum, so the contents of the bottle stay the same temperature.*

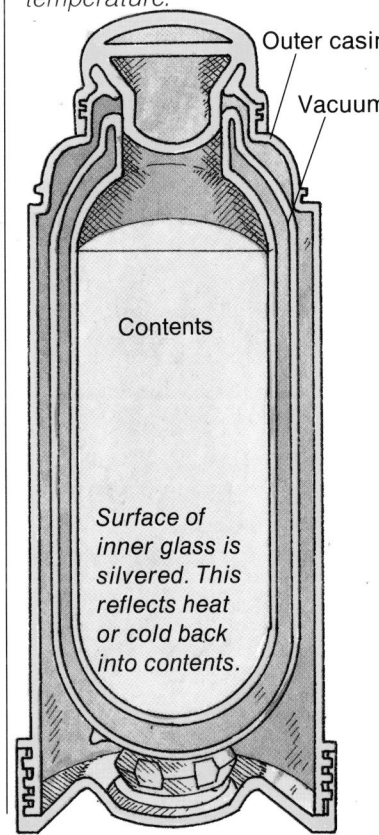

Outer casing

Vacuum

Contents

Surface of inner glass is silvered. This reflects heat or cold back into contents.

24. How long does it take the light from distant stars to reach us?

*There are some stars that are so far away that it takes years for their light to reach us. Light travels at a speed of 6 million million miles a year — we call this distance a **light year**. Our nearest star (apart from the Sun) is four light years away, but there are many other stars which are much, much further away.*

25. Could you take a photo of your insides?

Yes, we can take X-ray photographs of the inside of our bodies and the insides of other things, too.

X-rays are a special kind of light. When an X-ray photograph is taken, the rays pass through the softer parts of the body and show only the harder parts, such as the bones and some of the organs. Doctors can use X-rays to see where bones are broken. They can also be used in other ways, such as to find cracks in metal structures.

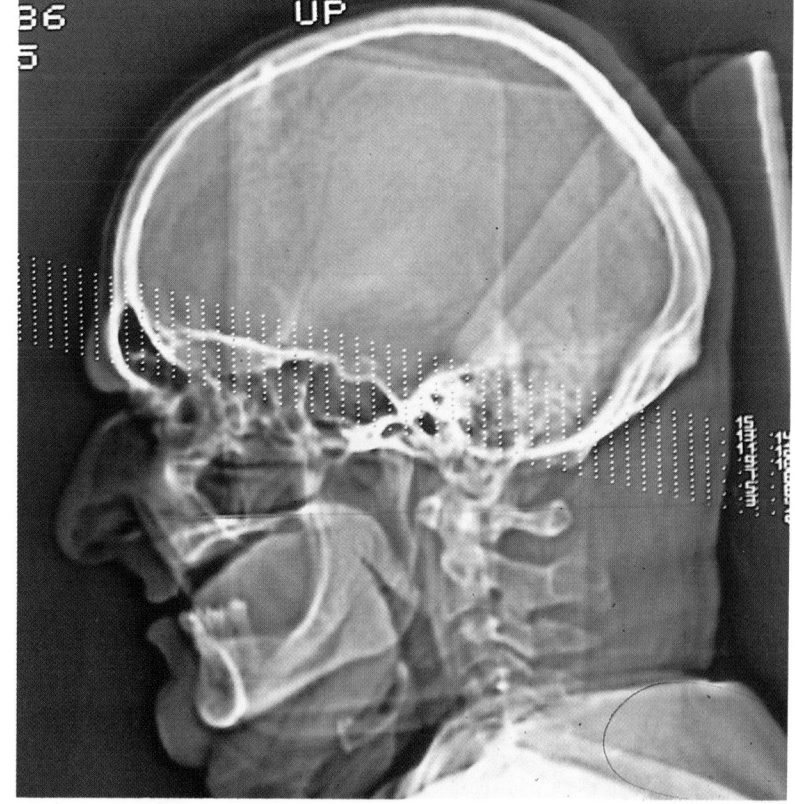

26. Do sounds make waves?

A sound is made when the molecules in a substance are made to vibrate. As the sound travels, the movement of the molecules spreads out like ripples on water. We call these ripples "sound waves."

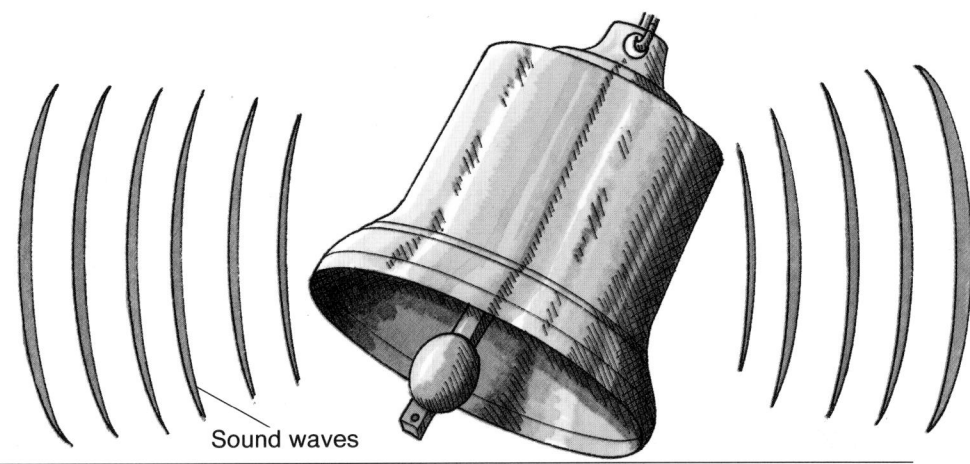

Sound waves

27. Could a nuclear power station actually melt?

A nuclear power station produces tremendous heat by the process known as nuclear fission (see page 11). This process, and the heat it makes, must be kept under control, or there could be a huge explosion. This is what happened at Chernobyl in the USSR in 1986, when a nuclear reactor exploded and caught fire. Normally, safety systems operate to stop this from happening. The heat from such an explosion could become so great that the core of the reactor could melt into the earth.

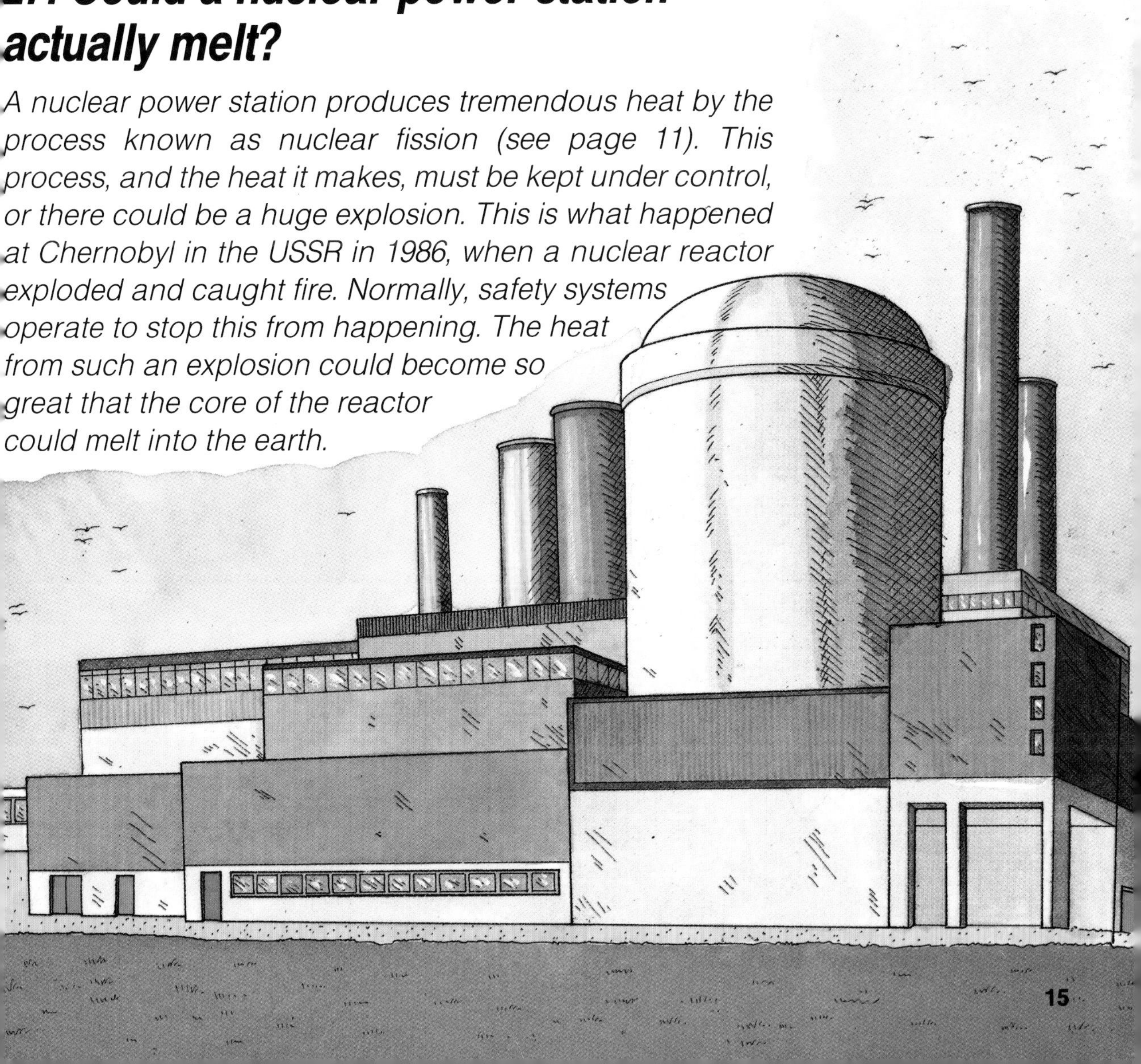

28. Is there a metal that is usually a liquid?

All metals become liquid when they are heated to the temperature at which they melt. Mercury is a metal that remains liquid at room temperature. It is a bright silver metal that is so runny it is often called "quicksilver." Because mercury expands easily with changes in temperature, it is used in thermometers and other scientific instruments.

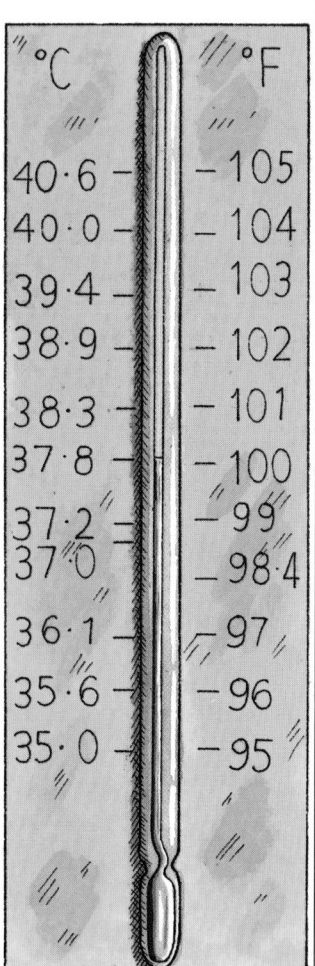

29. Are there dwarfs in space?

Yes, **White Dwarfs** are a kind of star. They develop from very large stars known as **Red Giants**. Eventually, these large stars lose their outer layer and shrink to become dwarf stars. So there are dwarfs and giants in space!

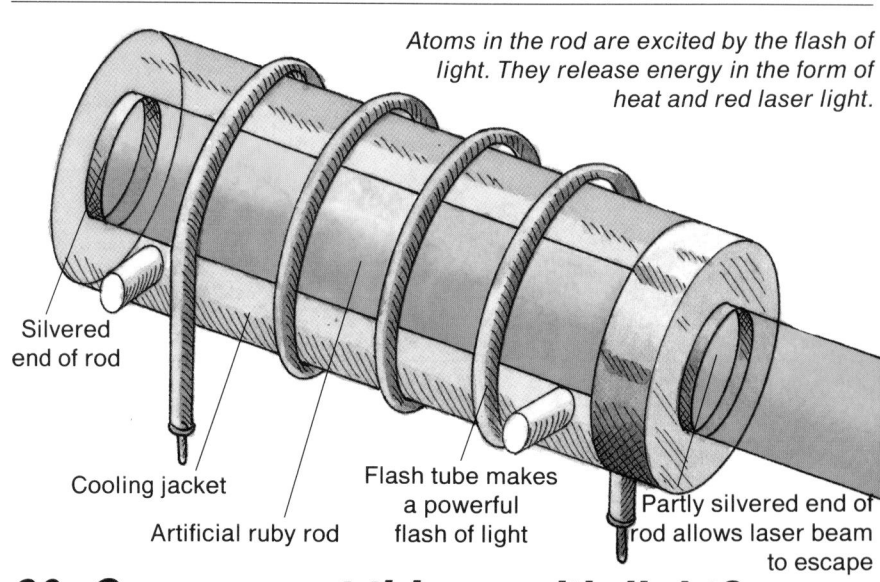

Atoms in the rod are excited by the flash of light. They release energy in the form of heat and red laser light.

Silvered end of rod

Cooling jacket

Artificial ruby rod

Flash tube makes a powerful flash of light

Partly silvered end of rod allows laser beam to escape

30. Can you cut things with light?

A **laser** (Light Amplification by Stimulated Emission of Radiation) produces a special beam of light which can actually cut things. Surgeons use them for particularly delicate operations. This is because lasers can cut without causing bleeding. Lasers can also be used in industry to cut or weld metal.

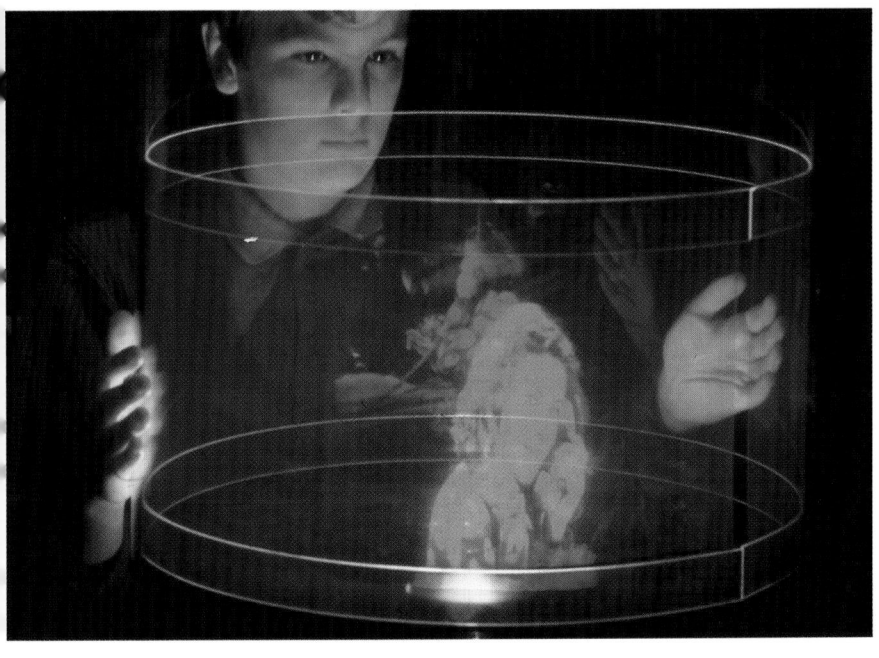

31. Can you make a three-dimensional picture?

*We can make three-dimensional pictures of objects. A picture like this is called a **hologram** and is made using a laser beam and a special photographic plate. A partly reflective mirror splits the beam in two — an **object** beam and a **reference** beam. The object beam reflects an image of the object onto the plate. The reference beam spreads out to form the background.*

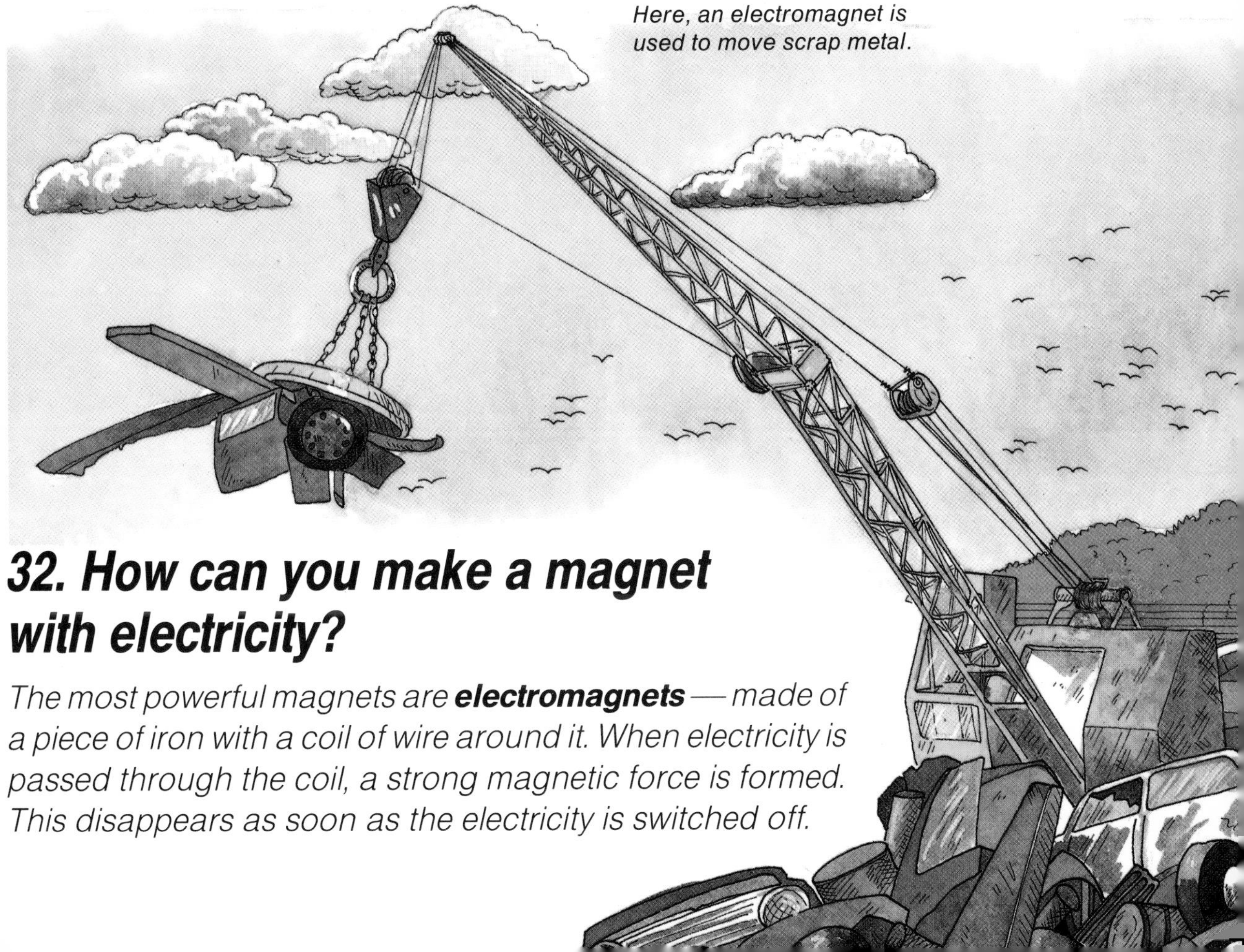

Here, an electromagnet is used to move scrap metal.

32. How can you make a magnet with electricity?

*The most powerful magnets are **electromagnets** — made of a piece of iron with a coil of wire around it. When electricity is passed through the coil, a strong magnetic force is formed. This disappears as soon as the electricity is switched off.*

33. Could you land an aircraft on an iceberg?

During World War II, a man called Geoffrey Pyke had an idea for building a floating airstrip from an iceberg. He created an artificial iceberg, made from wood pulp and ice. But it was not possible to make the runway long enough. Some of today's aircraft do not need long runways — so Pyke's iceberg could now be used, perhaps to provide runways for use by the offshore oil industry.

34. How much of an iceberg do you actually see?

An iceberg can stand as much as 88 feet above the surface of the sea and be up to 31 miles long. But, however large it is above the water, nine-tenths of it remain below the surface. This is because, although ice floats, it is very nearly the same density (weight for its volume) as ordinary liquid water. This means that most of it stays below the surface — where it cannot be seen.

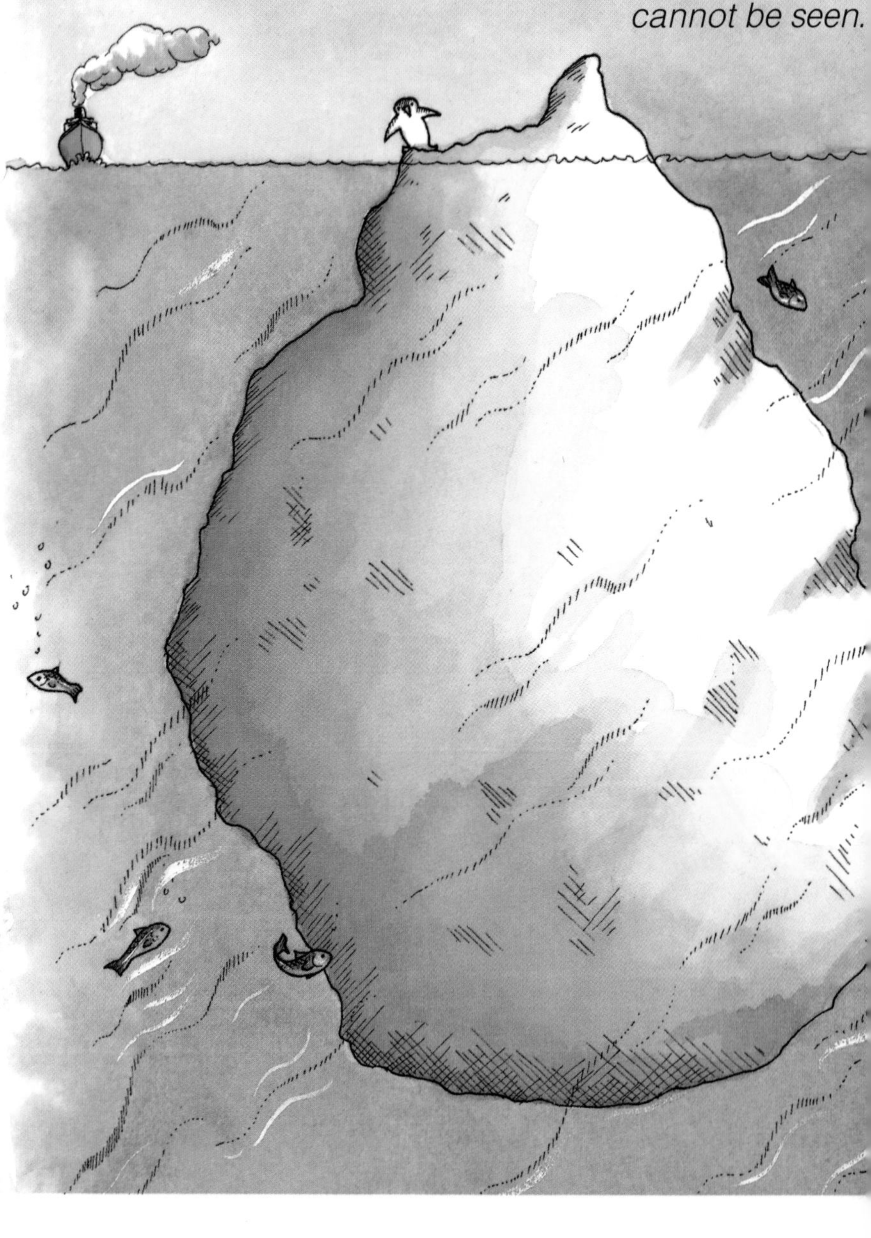

35. Can an aerosol spray make a hole in the atmosphere?

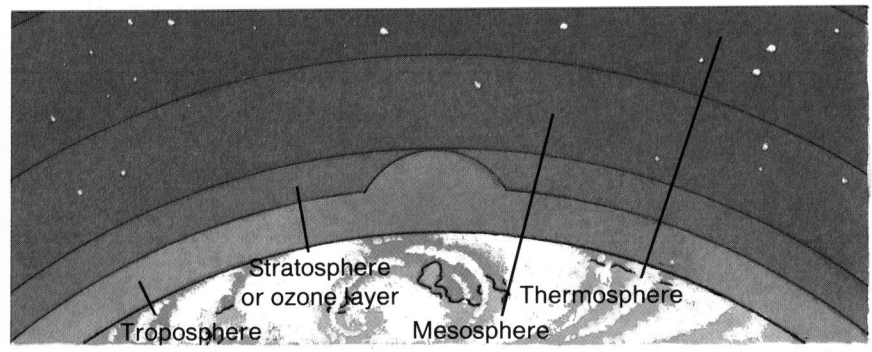

Stratosphere or ozone layer
Thermosphere
Troposphere
Mesosphere

About 6 miles from the Earth's surface is a layer of the atmosphere which protects us from the Sun's harmful ultraviolet rays. It contains a gas called ozone — so it is called the **ozone layer**. Scientists have found that it is being destroyed by a gas which arises from a group of chemicals (known as CFCs) that are sometimes used in aerosols.

36. Is plastic really made from oil?

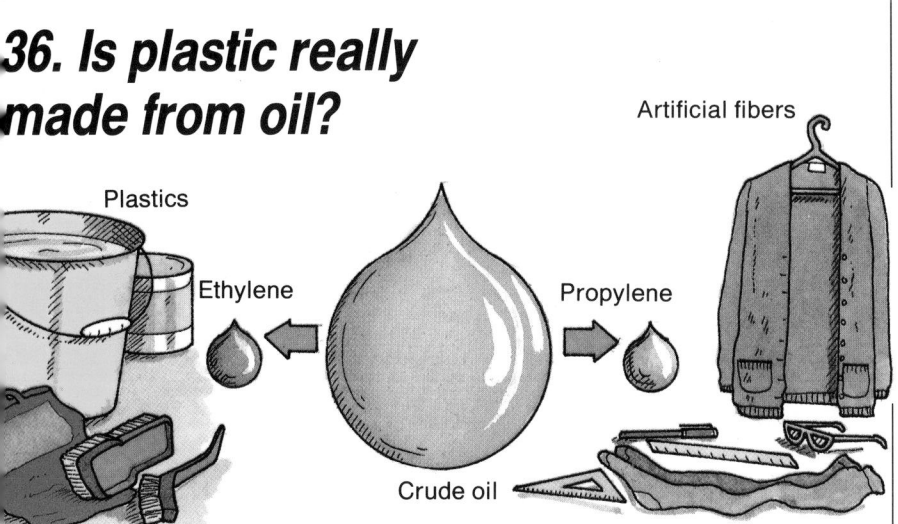

Plastics

Ethylene

Artificial fibers

Propylene

Crude oil

When heavy crude oil is heated it breaks up into different substances, called **fractions**. These include gases, gasoline and many others. Some fractions mix easily with each other and with other chemicals to make hundreds of different kinds of plastics. These can be used to make all sorts of things — from paint and pipes to fibers for cloth.

37. Have we received messages from Mars?

Yes, we have already had messages from Mars. They were not from Martians, but signals from spacecraft. The U.S. Space Program have landed two unmanned craft on Mars — Viking I and 2. These sent pictures and information about the atmosphere and soil of Mars. They showed a rocky surface, with ice at the poles, volcanoes, canyons, deserts, and craters where meteorites (see page 12) have struck the surface of Mars. There was no sign of life.

38. Will we ever be able to live on the Moon?

The Moon has no air. The only way anyone could live there would be in some sort of space station. This would have to contain air and water and protection from heat and cold. So far, no one has spent more than a few hours on the Moon itself, but people have lived for several months in space stations orbiting the Earth.

39. Is the Earth really a huge magnet?

If you have ever looked closely at a compass, you will have seen how the needle always points north. The compass needle is made of iron. It points north because it is attracted to the North Pole, just as it would be to the north pole of a magnet. This is because the Earth works like a huge electromagnet. Its core is made up of iron and nickel. As the Earth spins, its outer surface spins a little faster than this central core. This sets up a magnetic field — turning the Earth into a gigantic magnet.

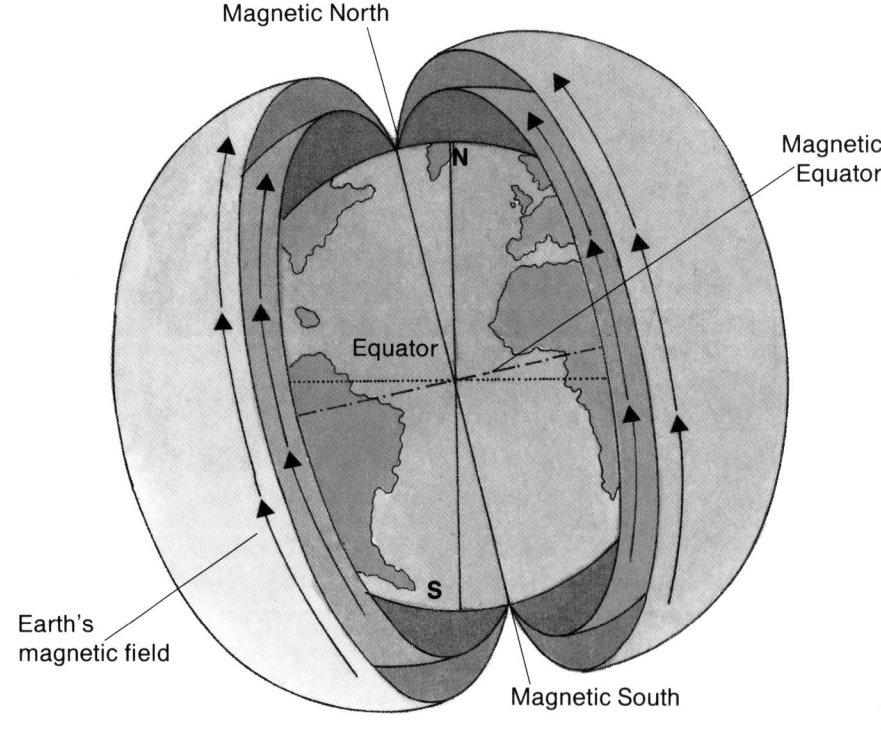

Magnetic North

Magnetic Equator

N

Equator

Earth's magnetic field

S

Magnetic South

40. Can a beam of light play records?

*Light is used to make and to play **compact discs**. When a disc is recorded, a master disc is made from specially coated glass. The sounds are converted into electrical signals, which direct a laser to cut pits into the disc. The discs we buy are copies of this master. The pits on the disc's surface are "read" by a laser stylus. The signals are then turned back into sounds by loudspeakers.*

41. Can you make gold?

*Alchemy developed in Arab countries and in Europe, in the Middle Ages. Some of the first scientists were **alchemists**. They were convinced that they could find a way of turning ordinary metals into gold. Of course, they were not success-ful, but they did make other useful discoveries.*

42. Does everything fall at the same speed?

Without air, everything would fall at the same speed, whatever it weighed, because of the pull of gravity. A feather only takes a long time to fall because it floats on the air.

43. How can clothes be whiter than white?

*People like to keep their white clothes looking really bright — but older fabrics soon lose their brightness. The makers of detergents have solved this problem by adding substances called **optical bleaches** to their powders. These are colorless dyes that reflect a kind of light called **ultraviolet light**. This makes the fabric appear to glow in sunlight.*

Before washing!

After washing!

44. Are Egyptian mummies really radioactive?

Egyptian mummies are slightly radioactive, as are all living things and their remains. Living things contain carbon. Some of this is radioactive carbon-14, taken in from the air. After death, no new carbon-14 is taken in. The carbon-14 in a dead body decays with time, and it does so at a constant rate. You can work out the age of a mummy by measuring its radioactivity and comparing it to that of a living thing.

45. Does radiation stay around for ever?

Radioactive substances give off harmful radiation. As they do so, they become less radioactive. Some substances do this very quickly — they may become quite safe in a few minutes or a few hours. Others take longer. Uranium remains radioactive for thousands of millions of years — maybe not for ever, but long enough!

Some nuclear waste remains radioactive for a long time. Because of this it is sometimes stored in special caverns such as this one, deep below the Earth's surface.

46. How can something grow just by getting hot?

When a substance is heated, the molecules that make it up vibrate and move apart from each other, so taking up more space. We call this **expansion**. Expansion can cause problems — for example, large structures such as bridges will expand slightly as a result of only small changes in temperature. They will buckle and bend if no allowance has been made for this. Spaces, called **expansion joints**, are built into bridges to prevent this happening.

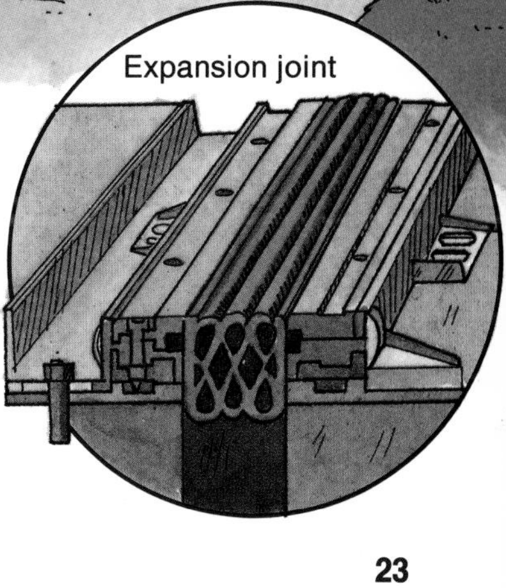

Expansion joint

47. Can you use salt to make ice cream?

Yes, in a machine that makes ice cream. A tub of ice cream is put in to a drum of ice. Salt is added to the ice. Unlike pure water, the salt/ice mixture needs to be colder than 32°F to stay frozen, and so the ice melts. The heat needed to melt the ice comes from the ice cream, which then freezes.

48. Can you really make electricity with a lemon?

Yes, you can use a lemon to make a home-made battery that works just like the ones you buy. Stick a piece of copper wire and a straightened-out paper clip into a lemon. If you connect these two wires, you will make an electrical circuit. Test this by touching the ends of both wires with your tongue. It will tingle as electricity passes through it.

In a real battery electricity is created by connecting two rods made of different metals, called **electrodes**, which have been placed in a liquid, called **electrolyte**. In your lemon battery the wires are the electrodes and the lemon juice is the electrolyte.

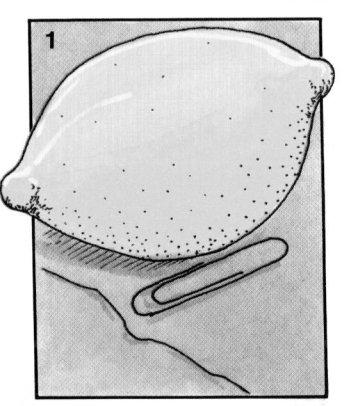

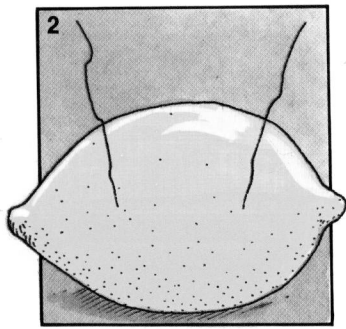

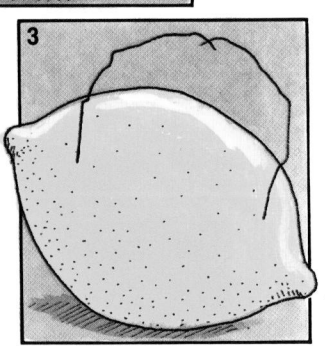

49. Can mountains grow?

The surface of the Earth never stays the same. The great plates that form the Earth's crust are always on the move. They move at a rate of $\frac{1}{2}$–$3\frac{1}{2}$ inches every year. Some plates collide and push up against each other along **destructive plate margins**. This is what has created the world's highest mountain range, the Himalayas. Two plates have collided and are forcing each other upward. This process is still going on and so the mountains are slowly growing.

50. Is it true that lightning never strikes twice in the same place?

No, it isn't true. Some places are struck again and again. Lightning tends to aim for the highest point around — so tall buildings, such as high office buildings, may be struck hundreds of times a year.

25

51. Is glass really made of sand?

Yes, most glass is made from **silica** sand, mixed with soda and limestone. This mixture is then heated to a very high temperature in a furnace. As the mixture cools, it solidifies into glass.

52. Who built the Giant's Causeway?

Legend has it that these strange columns off the coast of Northern Ireland were made by giants crossing the sea from Scotland. In fact, they were formed by an outpouring of lava from beneath the Earth's surface.

53. Can you skate on water?

Skaters do not actually move on ice, but on a thin layer of water. As skaters step out on the ice, their skates press down and melt the surface of the ice. This makes the ice slippery and the skates can slide along on it. Once the skater has moved on, the water freezes over again.

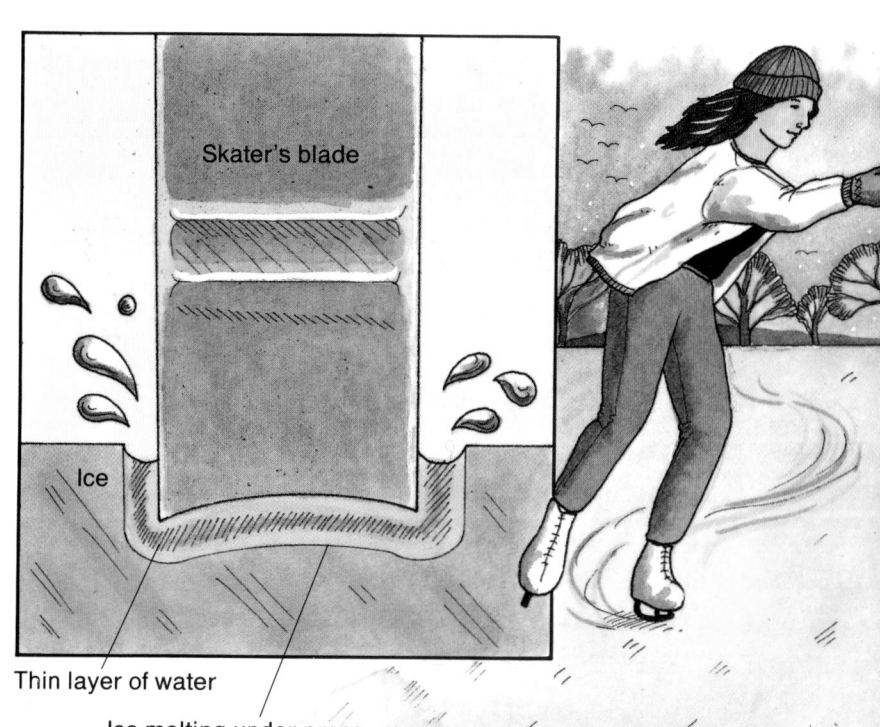

Skater's blade

Ice

Thin layer of water

Ice melting under pressure

54. How can acid rain from the sky?

Factory chimneys and car exhausts are continually releasing chemicals into the atmosphere. These chemicals mix with rain water to produce mild acids. In even small quantities, this acid rain can kill trees and crops, and pollute lakes. It also damages buildings and monuments, eating away at the stonework. This is a problem with structures of historic importance, such as this sandstone carving.

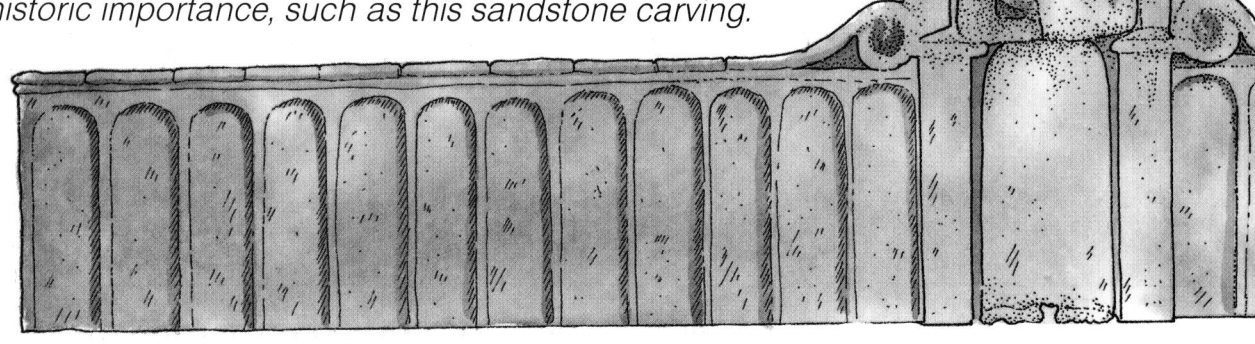

55. Are charcoal and diamonds really the same thing?

Charcoal and diamonds are both forms of carbon. They look different because their molecules are arranged differently. Charcoal is made from the partial burning of wood and is mostly carbon. Pure carbon is found naturally as graphite (the "lead" in pencils) and as diamonds. The latter are hard crystals which form when carbon is heated to high temperatures and cooled slowly under pressure.

Atomic structure of graphite

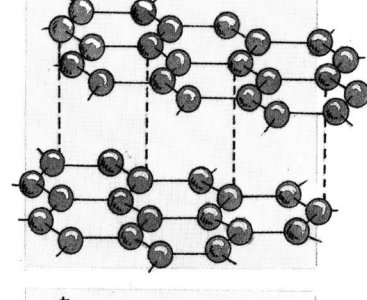

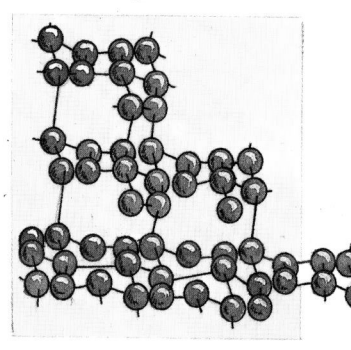

Atomic structure of diamond

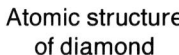

56. How long is a day on the planet Mercury?

The planet Mercury spins very slowly on its axis. The length of time it takes to spin once (one Mercury day) is the same as that taken by the Earth to spin 58.6 days. Other planets have different lengths of day. A Martian day lasts about as long as one of ours. A Jupiter day is less than half as long, while a Venus day lasts more than eight months!

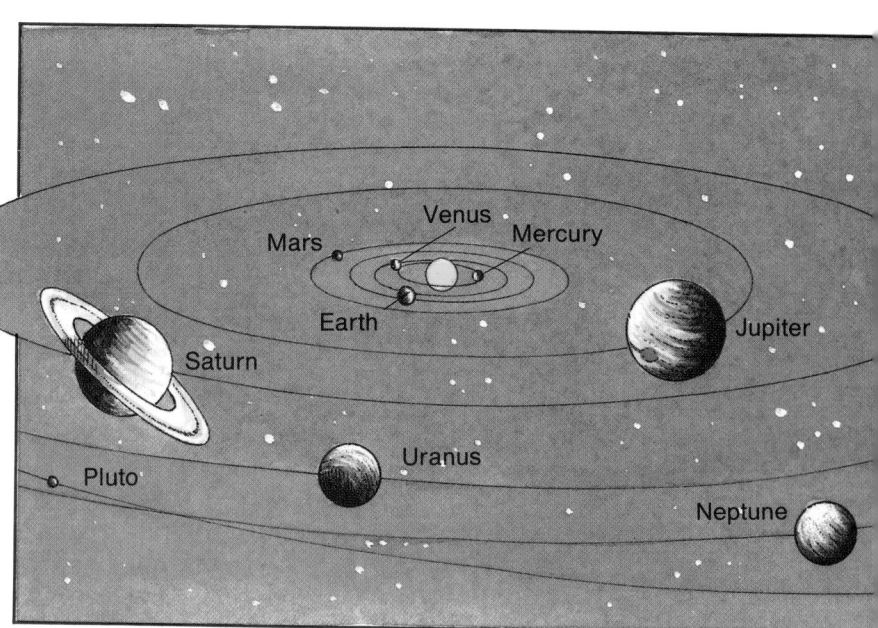

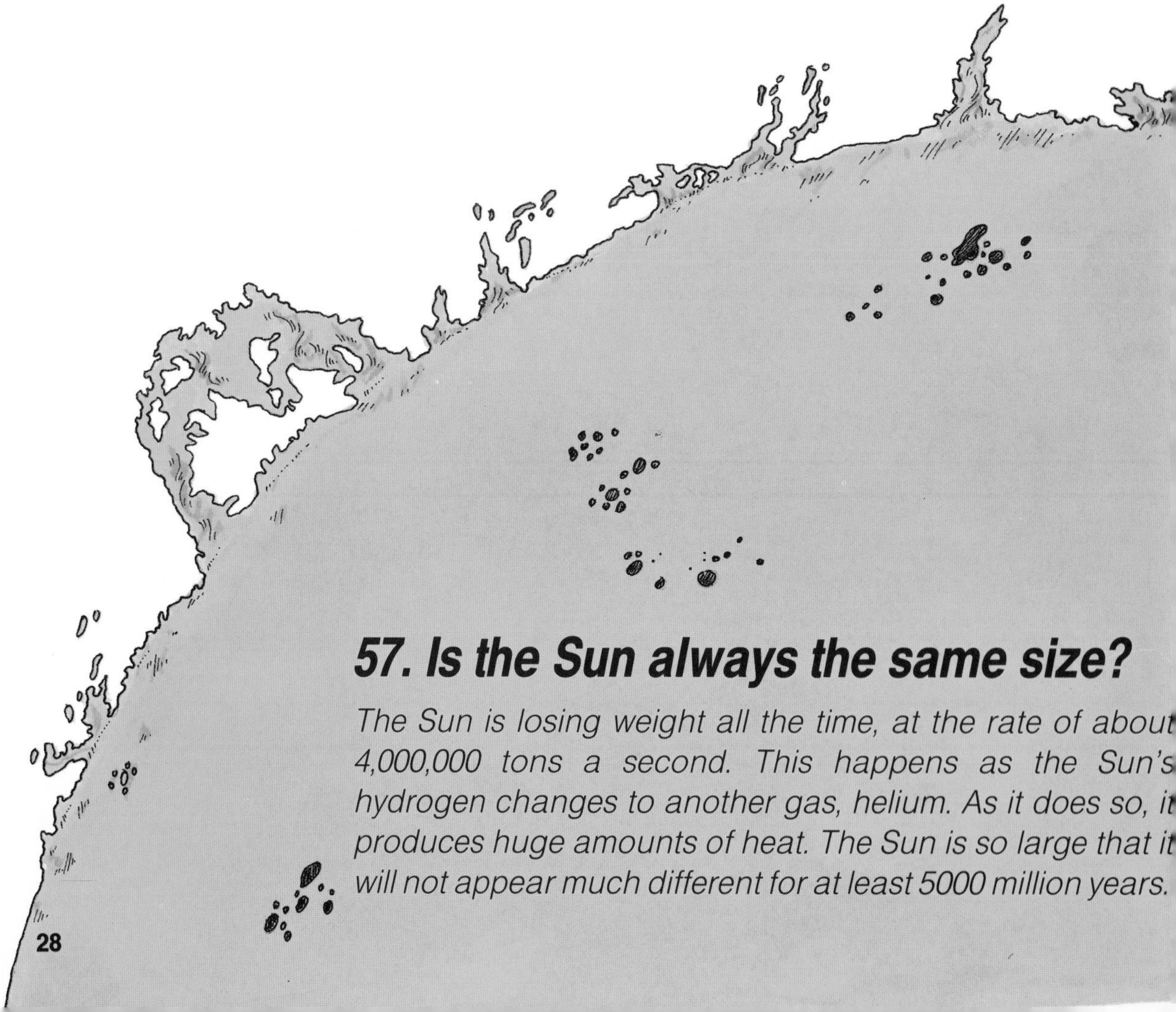

57. Is the Sun always the same size?

The Sun is losing weight all the time, at the rate of about 4,000,000 tons a second. This happens as the Sun's hydrogen changes to another gas, helium. As it does so, it produces huge amounts of heat. The Sun is so large that it will not appear much different for at least 5000 million years.

58. Can you use radio waves to look at the stars?

A radio telescope is not like an ordinary telescope — it is a huge satellite dish which picks up radio waves from far out in space. These waves come from the Sun and from other objects, including galaxies and the remains of stars that have exploded. The waves are recorded as a graph on tracing paper.

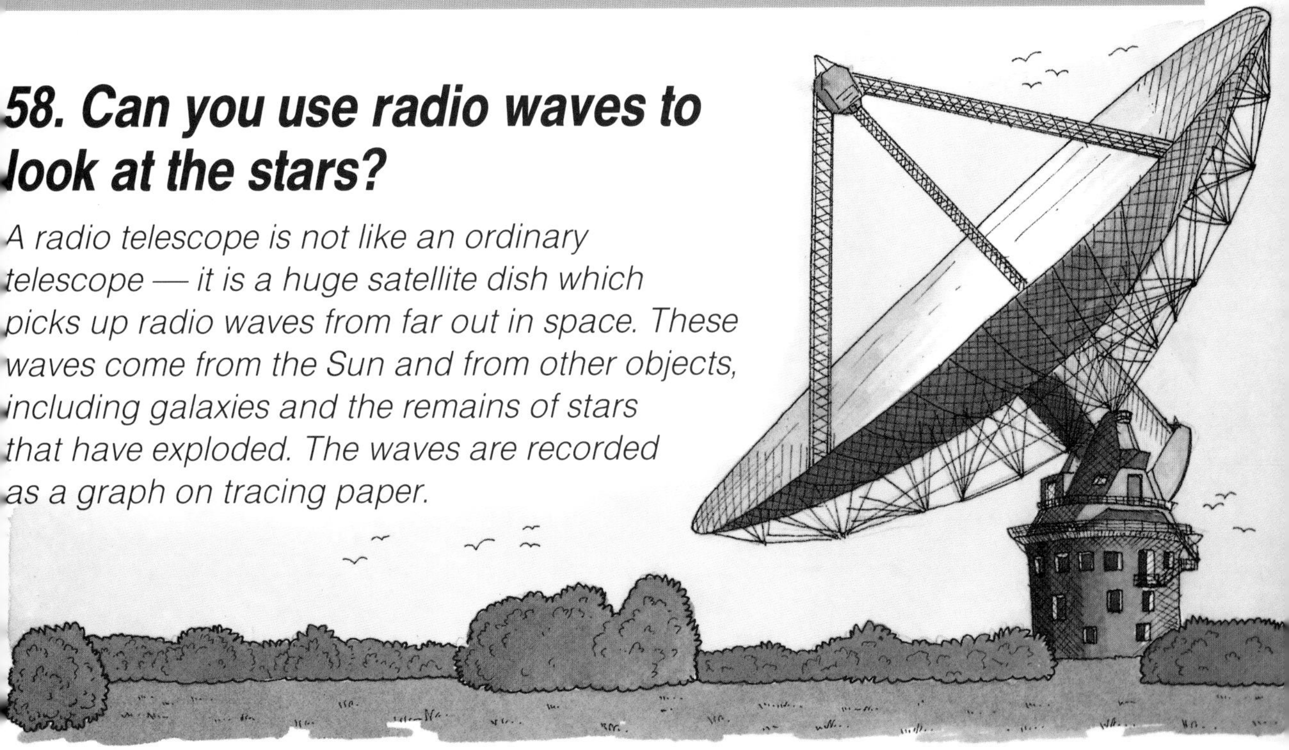

This is an infra-red photograph of New York City, taken from a satellite.

59. Can you tell if something is warm by looking at a photograph?

There is a kind of light, which we cannot see, called **infra-red radiation**. It gives off more heat than other light. Some photographic films can detect infra-red radiation. The temperatures of the objects photographed show up as different colors. Cool objects are blue or purple, hot ones white or red.

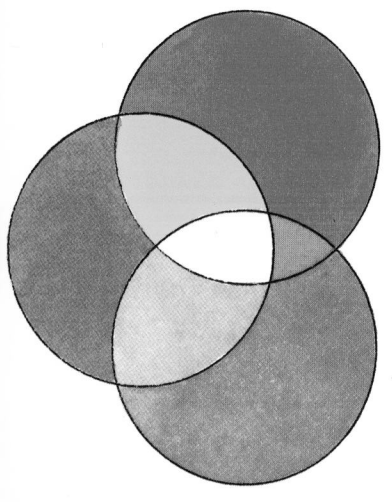

60. Can you make yellow from green and red?

*Yes, but you must use light and not paint. When you mix paints, you need just three **primary colors** — red, blue, and yellow — to make all the other colors. But if you are mixing colored light, the rules are quite different. The primary colors in light are red, green and blue. Red and green light make yellow, red and blue light make a purplish color called magenta and blue and green light make cyan, which is greenish blue. If all the colors of light are mixed together, they make colorless "white" light.*

61. Can a lightning rod really save a building in a storm?

Lightning rods work very simply. A strip of metal runs down the side of a tall building, from just above its highest point to the ground. When lightning strikes the rod, its electrical charge is carried along the metal strip to the ground, without doing any harm at all. The lightning is also drawn away from other buildings close to the lightning rod, making everyone safer.

One of the safest places to be during a storm is in a car. Lightning hits the outside of the metal car and runs into the earth. The people inside are not hurt.

62. How do you change the color of glass?

*The beautiful stained glass colors you see in church windows are created when the glass is being made. The mixture of sand and other substances that go to make up glass is called **frit**. In colored glass, certain metals are added to this frit before it is heated (see page 26). Copper and gold make red glass. Cobalt and cupric (copper) oxide make blue glass and chromium, copper and iron oxide make green glass. Yellow glass is made with cadmium or sulphur (which is not a metal).*

64. Is it possible to destroy something completely?

Matter can be destroyed, but it never vanishes, it changes into forms of energy. The hydrogen atoms of the Sun are being destroyed all the time. From them we get energy in the form of heat and light.

63. How do you use a laser to measure the distance between the Earth and the Moon?

A laser beam (see page 16), made up of millions of pulses of light a second, is sent to the Moon and bounces back off a reflector. Scientists measure exactly how long one pulse takes to make this journey. From this time they can calculate exactly how far away the Moon is.

65. Can we wear clothes made of plastic?

Yes, plastics are made up of hydrogen and carbon and come in all sorts of forms, including acrylic fibers and nylon. These are both used to make knitted garments — nylon is also used to make tights and stockings. Plastics called polyesters are used to make fabrics that do not stretch or lose their shape. A kind of plastic called cellulose acetate is used to make fabrics such as rayon.

66. What stops an aircraft from falling out of the sky?

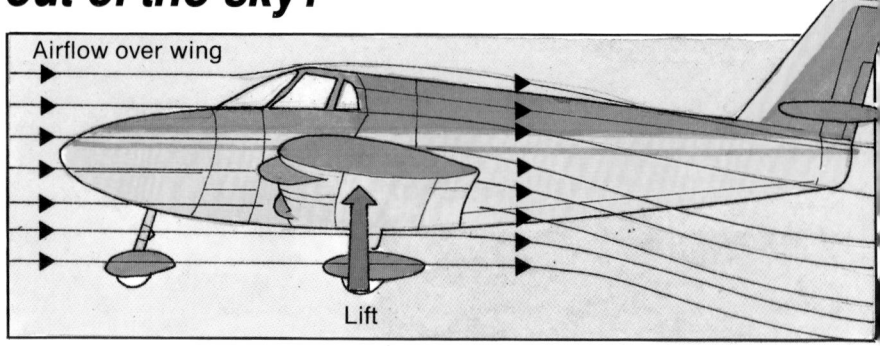

Airflow over wing

Lift

It is the movement of air around an aircraft's wings that keeps it in flight. The wings are a special shape. This shape is called an **aerofoil**. It has a curve on top and is flattened underneath. The wings are placed at a slight angle to the body of the aircraft. As the aircraft moves, the wings cut through the air. The air passing over the curved upper

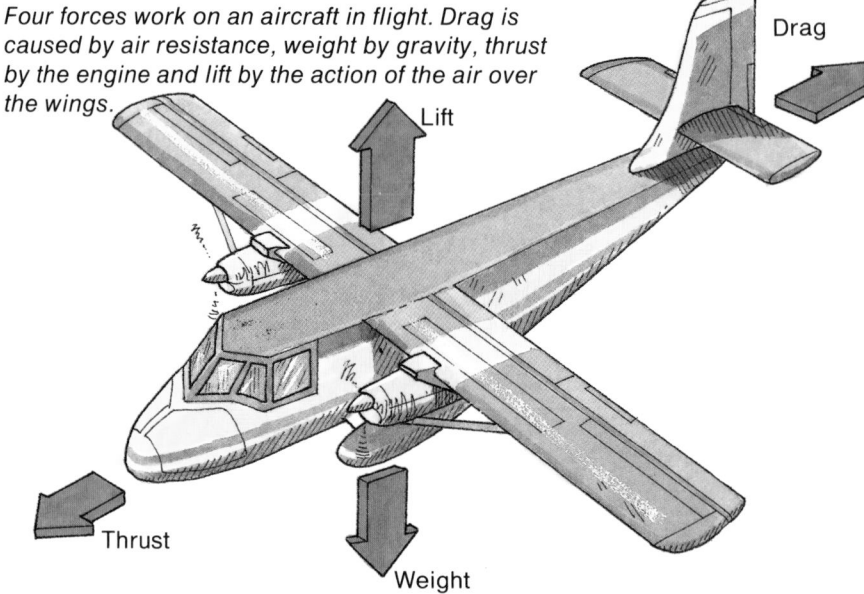

Four forces work on an aircraft in flight. Drag is caused by air resistance, weight by gravity, thrust by the engine and lift by the action of the air over the wings.

Drag

Lift

Thrust

Weight

surface of the wing moves faster than the air underneath the wing. This lowers the pressure above the wing and increases the pressure below the wing. This difference in air pressure lifts the aircraft. The "lift" the air provides must be enough to overcome the pull of gravity, which draws the aircraft down.

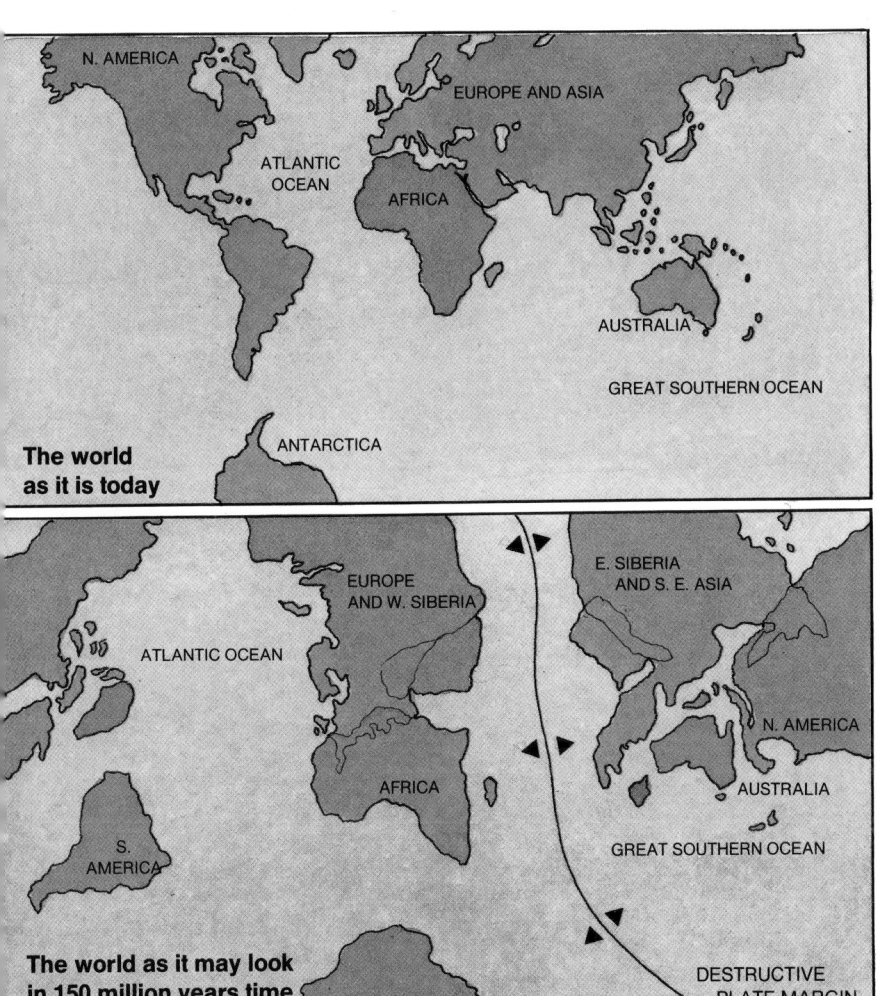

N. AMERICA

EUROPE AND ASIA

ATLANTIC OCEAN

AFRICA

AUSTRALIA

GREAT SOUTHERN OCEAN

The world as it is today

ANTARCTICA

EUROPE AND W. SIBERIA

E. SIBERIA AND S. E. ASIA

ATLANTIC OCEAN

N. AMERICA

AFRICA

AUSTRALIA

GREAT SOUTHERN OCEAN

S. AMERICA

The world as it may look in 150 million years time

ANTARCTICA

DESTRUCTIVE PLATE MARGIN

67. Will Asia really split in half one day?

The world has not always looked as it does today, and it will not stay the same for ever. The Earth's crust is made of huge plates. These are always on the move — slowly drifting apart or pushing together (see page 25). About 600 million years ago the world's continents, which are now separated by sea, were part of one great land mass. Over time they moved apart. This process is still taking place. There is a line across the Soviet Union where two plates meet. It runs through Lake Baikal — the deepest freshwater lake in the world. Scientists believe that, in 150 million years, these plates will have drifted apart and a sea will divide the land.

68. Can you keep water in a glass which is upside-down?

Try this. Pour water into a glass until it is nearly full. Put a piece of card over the top and hold it there. Turn the glass upside-down over a sink. Remove your hand from the card. The water should stay where it is. What happens is that the card bends outward slightly under the weight of the water. The air space inside the glass expands, lowering the air pressure. The pressure outside the glass is greater than the pressure inside.

33

69. What is talcum powder?

Talcum powder is made from soft white or green stone called **talc** or **soapstone**. Ground to powder, it is used in plaster, in paper-making, as "French chalk" in dressmaking, and to make talcum powder. Soapstone can also be carved to make ornaments.

70. Are all planets made of rock?

Our planet — the Earth — is made up of rock, but there are at least three planets in our solar system which are far less solid. One of these is Neptune, a greeny-blue planet far out in the solar system. Scientists think that it is made of gas, but it is too far away for anyone to know for sure. We know more about the larger planets: Jupiter (shown here) and Saturn. Their surfaces are made up of layers of gas. Inside, they are mainly liquid, with solid centers.

71. Does the world stay the same temperature?

Carbon dioxide "blanket"

Heat from earth cannot escape

Heat from Sun

The world is becoming warmer as the amount of the gas carbon dioxide in the air increases. Carbon dioxide forms when gas, oil, and coal are burned and from animal respiration. It acts like a blanket over the surface of the Earth, trapping the Sun's heat and warming our atmosphere. This is often referred to as the "greenhouse effect."

72. Does heat change things for ever?

Heat changes many things. We are familiar with the everyday process of cooking which changes food. Baking turns clay to hard brick. Burning can change substances to gas and, sometimes, ashes.

73. Are there really black holes in space?

"Black holes" form when a massive star has died. Smaller stars end their lives as "white dwarfs" (see page 16). Larger ones explode and become a patch of gas with a small, very dense **pulsar** in the center. The largest stars of all explode, then collapse and become very dense, pulling everything toward them. Not even light can escape. These are called "black holes."

INDEX

acid rain 27
acids 10
aerofoil 32
aerosol spray 19
air 4, 5, 13, 20, 21, 32
aircraft 5, 9, 18, 32
alchemy 21
Archimedes 6
atmosphere 19, 27, 35
atmospheric pressure 33
atoms 4, 7, 11, 31

big bang 12
black holes 35

carbon 27, 32
carbon-14 22
carbon dioxide 35
CFCs 19
chain reaction 11
charcoal 27
color 30, 31
compact discs 21
compounds 11
Concorde 9
cracking 8

Dead Sea 13
destructive plate margins 25, 33
detergents 22
diamonds 27
distillation columns 8

Earth 4, 5, 12, 19, 20, 25, 28, 31,
    33, 34, 35
electrical charge 7, 13, 30
electrical circuit 24
electrical signals 21
electricity 7, 17, 24
electromagnets 17, 20
electrons 4, 7
energy 7, 11, 16, 31
evaporation 13
expansion 23

fiber optic tubes 6
fibers 9, 19
fractions 19
frit 31

galaxies 12
gas 8, 19, 34, 35
Giant's Causeway 26
glass 9, 13, 21, 26, 31
gold 21
graphite 27
gravity 4, 21, 32
greenhouse effect 35

heat 7, 11, 15, 20, 23, 29, 31, 35

hologram 17
hydrogen 4, 28, 31, 32

ice 18, 26
ice cream 24
infra-red 29
iron 8, 17, 20

Jupiter 28, 34

lasers 16, 17, 21, 31
lava 26
lemon 24
light 6, 7, 8, 13, 14, 16, 21, 22, 29, 30,
    31, 35
lightning 25, 30
light year 14
liquid crystals 13

magnetism 17, 20
Mars 10, 19, 28
matter 31
mercury 16
Mercury 28
metal fatigue 5
metals 5, 7, 10, 11, 16, 21, 30, 31
meteorites 12, 19
meteors 12
mirror 7, 17
molecules 13, 15, 23, 27
Moon 4, 20, 31
mountains 25
mummies 22

nebulae 4
Neptune 28, 34
neutrons 4, 11
nickel 20
North Pole 20
nuclear fission 11, 15
nuclear power 11, 15
nucleus 4, 11

object beam 17
oil 8, 18, 19
optical bleaches 22
Orion 4
ozone layer 19

pig 8
planets 4, 10, 12, 28, 34
plastics 9, 19, 32
plates 25, 33
pressure 5, 13, 26, 27, 32, 33
primary colors 30
protons 4
pulsar 35
Pyke, Geoffrey 18

quicksilver 16

radioactivity 22, 23
radio waves 29
rainbow 8
Red Giants 16
reference beam 17

salt (sodium chloride) 11, 13, 24
salts 10
sand 8, 26, 31
Saturn 28, 34
shooting stars 12
soapstone 34
solar furnace 7
solar system 10, 34
sonic boom 9
sound 9, 15
space 4, 16, 35
space probes 10, 19
space station 20
stars 4, 12, 14, 16, 29, 35
steam 7, 11
Sun 7, 10, 19, 28, 31, 35
supersonic speed 9

talc 34
telecommunications 9
thermal radiation 7
thermometer 16
turbines 7, 11

ultraviolet light 19, 22
universe 4, 10, 12
uranium 11, 23

vacuum 13
Venus 10, 28
Viking spacecraft 19
volume 6

water 6, 13, 20, 26, 27, 33
White Dwarfs 16, 35

X-rays 14